DEATH

ann
ELIZABETH

Ann Elizabeth is the Founder & President of RealOron International Ministries, Inc.® | www.realoron.org

RealOron® is a ministry dedicated to the destruction of Biblical lack of knowledge, through evangelism and discipleship of all Nations.

Ann has pursued the heart of God and the Souls of Men throughout the years, with direct focus beginning at her supernatural encounter with the Lord in 2001.

Ann is a dynamic preacher, author, evangelist and teacher of the Word of God.

Death

Copyright ©2021

By Ann Elizabeth

No part of this book may be reproduced or transmitted in any form or by any means, electronic or mechanical, including photocopying and recording, or by any information storage or retrieval system, except as may be expressly permitted in writing by the author Ann Elizabeth. Requests for permission may be addressed at realoron@realoron.org.

ISBN Number – 9798716390799

All Scripture - King James Bible

DEATH

Death is something that happens, to all humanity.

Enjoy this book, as it will prepare you for the destiny you desire.

DEATH

○ WHAT IS THE DEFINITION OF DEATH?

DEATH IS THE END OF ONE'S LIFE, ON EARTH.

HEBREWS 13:14

"For here have we no continuing city, but we seek one to come."

○ THE LORD DESIRES FOR ALL HUMANITY, TO INHERIT ETERNAL LIFE.

EZEKIEL 18:23

"Have I any pleasure at all that the wicked should die? Saith the Lord God: and not that he should return from his ways, and live?"

JOHN 3:16-18

"For God so loved the world, that he gave his only begotten Son, that whosoever believeth in him should not perish, but have everlasting life.

[17] For God sent not his Son into the world to condemn the world; but that the world through him might be saved.

[18] He that believeth on him is not condemned: but he that believeth not is condemned already, because he hath not believed in the name of the only begotten Son of God."

JOHN 6:40

"This is the will of him that sent me, that every one which seeth the Son, and believeth on him, may have everlasting life: and I will raise him up at the last day."

O DEATH IS AN EVENT, EVERY PERSON WILL FACE.

PSALM 89:48

"What man *is he that* liveth, and shall not see death? Shall he deliver his soul from the hand of the grave? Selah."

JOB 5:26

"Thou shalt come to *thy* grave in a full age, like as a shock of corn cometh in in his season."

ECCLESIASTES 9:5

"For the living know that they shall die: but the dead know not anything, neither have they any more a reward; for the memory of them is forgotten."

O DEATH IS AN EVENT BOTH RICH AND POOR, WILL FACE.

LUKE 16:19-31

"There was a certain rich man, which was clothed in purple and fine linen, and fared sumptuously every day:

[20] And there was a certain beggar named Lazarus, which was laid at his gate, full of sores,

[21] And desiring to be fed with the crumbs which fell from the rich man's table: moreover the dogs came and licked his sores.

²² And it came to pass, that the beggar died, and was carried by the angels into Abraham's bosom: the rich man also died, and was buried;

²³ And in hell he lift up his eyes, being in torments, and seeth Abraham afar off, and Lazarus in his bosom.

²⁴ And he cried and said, Father Abraham, have mercy on me, and send Lazarus, that he may dip the tip of his finger in water, and cool my tongue; for I am tormented in this flame.

²⁵ But Abraham said, Son, remember that thou in thy lifetime receivedst thy good things, and likewise Lazarus evil things: but now he is comforted, and thou art tormented.

²⁶ And beside all this, between us and you there is a great gulf fixed: so that they which would pass from hence to you cannot; neither can they pass to us, that would come from thence.

²⁷ Then he said, I pray thee therefore, father, that thou wouldest send him to my father's house:

²⁸ For I have five brethren; that he may testify unto them, lest they also come into this place of torment.

²⁹ Abraham saith unto him, They have Moses and the prophets; let them hear them.

³⁰ And he said, Nay, father Abraham: but if one went unto them from the dead, they will repent.

³¹ And he said unto him, If they hear not Moses and the prophets, neither will they be persuaded, though one rose from the dead."

○ DEATH CAN OCCUR; SUDDENLY.

JOB 21:13

"They spend their days in wealth, and in a moment go down to the grave."

JOB 34:20

"In a moment shall they die, and the people shall be troubled at midnight, and pass away: and the mighty shall be taken away without hand."

○ AFTER DEATH, ALL PEOPLE FACE GOD'S JUDGMENT; GOD'S RIGHTEOUS SENTENCE ON THEIR LIFE.

HEBREWS 9:27

"It is appointed unto men once to die, but after this the judgment."

○ THERE ARE TWO LOCATIONS IN ETERNITY.

1. HEAVEN.

HEAVEN IS A BEAUTIUL PLACE, PREPARED FOR THE PEOPLE WHO LOVE AND OBEY JESUS CHRIST.

JOHN 14:2-3

"In my Father's house are many mansions: if it were not so, I would have told you. I go to prepare a place for you.

3 And if I go and prepare a place for you, I will come again, and receive you unto myself; that where I am, there ye may be also."

HEAVEN IS FOR THE PEOPLE WHO HAD THEIR SINS REMOVED, BY THE BLOOD OF JESUS; AND DO THE WILL OF GOD.

REVELATION 22:14

"Blessed *are* they that do his commandments, that they may have right to the tree of life, and may enter in through the gates into the city."

HEAVEN IS FOR THE PEOPLE, WHO REPENTED AND WERE CONVERTED TO CHRIST, WITH PURITY AND RIGHTEOUSNESS IN THEIR DAILY LIVES.

ACTS 3:19

"Repent ye therefore, and be converted, that your sins may be blotted out, when the times of refreshing shall come from the presence of the Lord."

MATTHEW 18:3

"Except ye be converted, and become as little children, ye shall not enter into the kingdom of heaven."

REVELATION 21:7

"He that overcometh shall inherit all things; and I will be his God, and he shall be my son."

2. HELL.

HELL IS FOR THE PEOPLE WHO REJECTED THE LOVE, FORGIVENESS AND TRANSFORMATION ALMIGHTY GOD OFFERED TO THEM; THROUGH JESUS CHRIST.

PSALM 21:8-9

"Thine hand shall find out all thine enemies: thy right hand shall find out those that hate thee.

⁹ Thou shalt make them as a fiery oven in the time of thine anger: the Lord shall swallow them up in his wrath, and the fire shall devour them."

JUDE 1:7

"Even as Sodom and Gomorrha, and the cities about them in like manner, giving themselves over to fornication, and going after strange flesh, are set forth for an example, suffering the vengeance of eternal fire."

HELL IS FOR THE PEOPLE, WHO REFUSED TO STOP SINNING.

AMOS 9:10

"All the sinners of my people shall die by the sword, which say, The evil shall not overtake nor prevent us."

JOB 7:9

"As the cloud is consumed and vanisheth away: so he that goeth down to the grave shall come up no more."

JOB 24:19

"Drought and heat consume the snow waters: so doth the grave those which have sinned."

JOB 33:22

"Yea, his soul draweth near unto the grave, and his life to the destroyers."

ISAIAH 26:14

"The dead will not live, the departed spirits will not rise; Therefore You have punished and destroyed them, And You have wiped out all remembrance of them."

MATTHEW 13:41-42

"The Son of man shall send forth his angels, and they shall gather out of his kingdom all things that offend, and them which do iniquity;

42 And shall cast them into a furnace of fire: there shall be wailing and gnashing of teeth."

GALATIANS 5:19-21

"The works of the flesh are manifest, which are these; Adultery, fornication, uncleanness, lasciviousness,

20 Idolatry, witchcraft, hatred, variance, emulations, wrath, strife, seditions, heresies,

21 Envyings, murders, drunkenness, revellings, and such like: of the which I tell you before, as I have also told you in time past, that they which do such things shall not inherit the kingdom of God."

1 CORINTHIANS 6:9-10

"Know ye not that the unrighteous shall not inherit the kingdom of God? Be not deceived: neither fornicators, nor idolaters, nor adulterers, nor effeminate, nor abusers of themselves with mankind,

10 Nor thieves, nor covetous, nor drunkards, nor revilers, nor extortioners, shall inherit the kingdom of God."

REVELATION 21:8

"The fearful, and unbelieving, and the abominable, and murderers, and whoremongers, and sorcerers, and idolaters, and all liars, shall have their part in the lake which burneth with fire and brimstone: which is the second death."

⊙ JESUS CHRIST WARNS HUMANITY; OF HELL.

1 SAMUEL 2:6

"The LORD killeth, and maketh alive: he bringeth down to the grave, and bringeth up."

MATTHEW 10:28

"Fear not them which kill the body, but are not able to kill the soul: but rather fear him which is able to destroy both soul and body in hell."

⊙ NOT ONE PERSON REMAINS ON THE EARTH, ALL DEPART.

1. THE PRIDEFUL DIE.

ISAIAH 14:9-11

"Hell from beneath is moved for thee to meet *thee* at thy coming: it stirreth up the dead for thee, *even* all the chief ones of the earth; it hath raised up from their thrones all the kings of the nations.

10All they shall speak and say unto thee, Art thou also become weak as we? Art thou become like unto us?

11Thy pomp is brought down to the grave, *and* the noise of thy viols: the worm is spread under thee, and the worms cover thee."

2. THE RIGHTEOUS DIE.

2 CHRONICLES 34:28

"Behold, I will gather thee to thy fathers, and thou shalt be gathered to thy grave in peace."

ISAIAH 57:1

"The righteous perisheth, and no man layeth it to heart: and merciful men are taken away, none considering that the righteous is taken away from the evil to come."

PROVERBS 14:32

"The wicked is driven away in his wickedness: but the righteous hath hope in his death."

PSALM 116:15

"Precious in the sight of the Lord, is the death of his saints."

REVELATION 14:13

"I heard a voice from heaven saying unto me, Write, Blessed are the dead which die in the Lord from henceforth: Yea, saith the Spirit, that they may rest from their labours; and their works do follow them."

I PRAY, YOU CHOOSE HEAVEN.

ENJOY YOUR JOURNEY.

ANN ELIZABETH

REALORON FOUNDER & PRESIDENT

REFERENCE: THE HOLY BIBLE (KING JAMES VERSION).

WWW.REALORON.ORG

WWW.REALORON.ORG

WWW.REALORON.ORG

WWW.REALORON.ORG

WWW.REALORON.ORG

www.ingramcontent.com/pod-product-compliance
Lightning Source LLC
Chambersburg PA
CBHW060950130726
48001CB00003B/1146